Naming the Leper

BARATARIA POETRY

Ava Leavell Haymon, Series Editor

Naming the Leper

POEMS

Christopher Lee Manes

LOUISIANA STATE UNIVERSITY PRESS
BATON ROUGE

Published by Louisiana State University Press
Copyright © 2020 by Christopher Lee Manes

LSU Press Paperback Original
First printing

Designer: Breanne Plaisance
Typeface: Whitman
Printer and binder: LSI

Library of Congress Cataloging-in-Publication Data

Names: Manes, Christopher Lee, author.
Title: Naming the leper : poems / Christopher Lee Manes.
Description: Baton Rouge : Louisiana State University Press, [2020] |
Series: Barataria poetry
Identifiers: LCCN 2019040480 (print) | LCCN 2019040481 (ebook) |
    ISBN 978-0-8071-7112-7 (paperback) | ISBN 978-0-8071-7328-2
(pdf) | ISBN 978-0-8071-7329-9 (epub)
Subjects: LCSH: Leprosy—Patients—Poetry. | LCGFT: Poetry.
Classification: LCC PS3613.A53668 N36 2020 (print) | LCC PS3613.
    A53668 (ebook) | DDC 811/.6—dc23
LC record available at https://lccn.loc.gov/2019040480
LC ebook record available at https://lccn.loc.gov/2019040481

To my parents, John and Patricia

to my nieces, Harper and Iris

and to Sadie Morgan Spencer, of blessed memory,
11 November 1918 to 11 January 2016

Contents

Preface

In response to public hysteria about what was then named leprosy in the port city of New Orleans, a temporary shelter for "lepers" was established, in 1894, near Carville, Louisiana. To maintain secrecy and protect the first seven patients, a rumor was propagated that the property was to be an ostrich farm. More than a decade later, the property was purchased by the state of Louisiana, and it became the unofficial "leprosarium" for the continental United States. The federal government purchased it in 1920, and management and control was turned over to the United States Public Health Service the following year. In this book, the poet uses the word "leper" when writing about the years during which it was so named, but uses the contemporary and much less stigmatizing term "Hansen's disease" for the years after that name became the norm.

No matter their class, social standing, wealth or the lack of it, people diagnosed as "lepers" became outcasts, just as had the "lepers" in the Bible, and a deep shame enveloped their families. Government regulations required that the adult or child so diagnosed must either immediately present themselves at the leprosarium or be taken from the family home by force. These actions were often completed in the dead of night, the apprehended person perhaps never spoken of by their family again, often never seen again, and certainly not released without a medical discharge. The biblical "lepers" are now thought to have suffered, not with Hansen's disease, but from other skin disorders, such as psoriasis. In addition, despite accumulating medical evidence to the contrary, leprosy was considered highly contagious.

In 1941, a sulfone drug was first used experimentally. Over the next years, different drug treatments were explored, and found to be successful. Some residents were treated and released, some chose never to leave Carville because of disfigurement and nerve damage, and some did not go home again for reasons of their own. By the 1950s, Carville became a world center for research into Hansen's disease. The last two patients exited Carville in 2015.

Poet Christopher Manes descends from a family disrupted by this disease, by the mechanical response that it triggered, and by the continuing distortion of family relationships understandable after such trauma. Manes has composed this documentary poetry (sometimes called "docupoetry") using material from his family's stories, some of them contradictory as is always the case. He utilizes "found language" from a great trove of letters from family members in Carville and out, medical reports, government regulations, legal documents, and newspaper reports. The extensive notes at the end of this book reveal specific sources for individual poems, many archived, but some of which are letters and papers in the possession of the poet and other family members.

The names of patients, family members on the "outside," and other letter writers are numerous and necessarily confusing. The confusion is increased by the fact that when victims of Hansen's disease were first detained at Carville, they often chose aliases. In the notes at the end, the poet provides a family tree to aid the reader.

It is our hope that this book of documentary poetry will add human faces to the story of the National Hansen's Disease Center in Carville, Louisiana.

Ava Leavell Haymon

ACKNOWLEDGMENTS

The genesis of *Naming the Leper* is a 2001 chapbook that I wrote in the creative writing department at the University of Louisiana at Lafayette and my 2003 master's thesis, both of which were entitled "Regardez." In its Spring 2002 issue, the *Southwestern Review* published a poem I wrote named "Leprosy Annotated from Public Health Policy to Personal Narrative" that equally inspired the writings of this book, as did my essay "Regarding Carville: The Letters of Norbert and Edmond Landry," published in the Summer 2003 issue of *Louisiana History*.

Grateful acknowledgment is made to the editors and professors at the University of Louisiana at Lafayette who made these original published works possible, including but not limited to Drs. Vaughan Baker, Judith Gentry, Julia Frederick, John Laudun, Carl A. Brasseaux, Marcia Gaudet, Darrell Bourque, Willard "Skip" Fox, and Jerry McGuire.

Matthew Zapruder also read a much earlier version of some of these poems during a Juniper Summer Writing Institute at the University of Massachusetts at Amherst in 2005. Even now, I appreciate and use his feedback in my poetry.

I am grateful to Annette Dussett for reading an earlier draft of this book and discussing with me her mother, Sadie Morgan Spencer.

I thank Brad St. Marie for researching St. Peter's Catholic Church records and confirming the church documents regarding Georges-Charles Landry.

Elizabeth Schexnyder, curator of the National Hansen's Disease Museum, graciously answered my questions regarding some of the historical details in the preface and notes.

Special thanks to Patricia Smith Merriwether and my mother, Patricia Manes, for encouraging me to return to my initial work on "leprosy" and to look at it anew after the death of my friend Brian Cross in 2017. This book could not have been written, and in some parts rewritten, without their support.

For the opportunity to read a revised version of these poems to the Dallas Poets Community on January 5, 2018, my sincerest gratitude to Melanie Pruit and Ann Howells.

To MaryKatherine Callaway and Ava Leavell Haymon, thank you for the opportunity of a lifetime.

Naming the Leper

Tall Tales Grow Limbs, My Mother Said

In the beginning the word lived among us
    An American mindset, public health policy, and finally flesh
But I was nursing, she said, when it first learned to hiss
    And move down transoms over my crib
Adapted to syllables, it had breath and could rattle
    The underbelly of particulars from cattle milk
Which we sipped

No, that can't be it. It must have come from the fish
    Become the word Terville choked on when he swallowed
The fish bone that split his esophagus. At the same time
    Carville was said to breed ostriches
And the word took on feathers before anyone corrected it

In the name of my kin
    I listened, changed skins, and grew stilts
To reach the height of the tallest tree, where their spirits nested
    And the word dwelt in the wind

LIVING DEAD

The Book of Names

These are the children of Terville and Lucie by order of birth:
    Edmond, Norbert, Charlie, Marie, Albert, and Amelie
This is the order they died:
    Charlie, Norbert, Edmond, Amelie, Marie, and Albert

These are the children of Edmond and Claire:
    Leonide and Wilbert
This is the order they died:
    Wilbert and Leonide

These are the names of the women
    Who told my mother the family's stories:
Sadie Morgan Spencer and Zenobia Racely

These are the last names of doctors who participated in
    Norbert, Edmond, Amelie, Marie, and Albert's incarcerations:
Mouton, Sabatier, Johns, Denney, Mengis, Faget, and Johansen

These are the names of the 1917 surgeon general
    And secretary of the treasury:
Rupert Blue and William Gibbs McAdoo
    Who carried out Public Law 64-299

These are the names
    Norbert, Edmond, and Amelie chose in confinement:
James Jackson, Gabe Michael, and Emma Lee Michael

This is the place Norbert, Edmond, Amelie, Marie, and Albert
    Were forced to live and to die: United States Marine Hospital
No. 66, otherwise known as Carville

Public Law

These were the procedures
    Concerning leprosy eruptions and ostrich farms in 1917:
When a diagnosis was suspected
    In accordance with paragraph 32.86
The patient in question could not be
    In contact with people on the street and in the stores
And, if the diagnosis was confirmed,
    A patient had to volunteer admittance to Carville

The way ostrich feathers are clipped begins at six months old
    When the bird is as tall as its parents,
Has a curved neck, small head, humped back, paddled toes,
    And an ungainly walk. From that time forth, every six months
The feathers are clipped and sold
    At eight feet tall, an ostrich's single leap covers twenty-five feet

Public health employees at Carville earned additional pay
    For working with lepers, though by 1906
The medical community believed it to be the least contagious
    Of all diseases. These were the patients never compelled
To live under armed guard, without the right to vote, to marry
    Or to live where they might:
Those with smallpox and tuberculosis

This House Is Sick, Sadie Told My Mother

In the 1980s, ironing Claire's laundry at 24 dollars a week,
    Sadie remembered all this:
Lucie Landry thought the house was diseased
    And her memories flapped like a fish
Her husband choked on a fish bone
    On the bed where she birthed her children
When he gurgled "Amelie," she said, "Let him go"

In the old photo, Lucie sits on the porch swing wanting to know
    What it was like to lie on wide planks like the cypress boards
On which she buried her sons Norbert and Edmond
    Or in the copper-lined casket her daughter Amelie requested
Because she didn't want a big box
    On the porch, it smelled of dirt and pine
Rocks and buttercups, pink and white

Before entering Carville, Albert and Marie drove their mother
    To Texas. Much of the trip was over rivers, mud, ruts, dust
And sometimes pavement. After many years of death, in the days
    When Washington Street still connected New Iberia
To Lafayette, Lucie forgot she was living

Sadie said after Lucie was alone
    She continued to remember the birth of her babies
How it rained inside the house, even in her eyes
    She strained to see until someone held a bucket over her face
She tried to speak, but language sifted
    Through splinters and concrete

From the Grave, Lucie Orchestrates Her Memories

Lucie remembers her third-born, Charlie
    I didn't know, she says, or thinks she does
That a child could be so cold
    There wasn't even time to embalm him
I just wrapped him in sheets, however many I could
    I wanted him to stay warm. Wanted him to sleep

The ground swelled for days adjusting to the space of him
    Somewhere between bone and boon, skeleton and prayer
I thought he would rise. I half-hoped to hear him cry
    So that I could bury my hands into the dirt and hold him
Then the ground began to shift, constrict
    And I knew he was giving in to it

Amelie is the one I think of after him
    From Carville my daughter cried
Out of her *button-hole mouth*. She couldn't speak
    But I knew she wanted to say "Mommy"
Emaciated, a chatter of bones, she reached for my hand
    Shaking like the day she was born

Only the week before, it seemed, I had asked her
    To make out a list of things she wanted for Christmas:
Cakes and writing pens, clothes, friends, and earrings
    Now, again, she has written a list
Mama, it begins, I want a comfortable gown, lavender or mint,
    And a copper-lined casket

EDMOND, WRITING UNDER HIS CARVILLE NAME
GABE MICHAEL, IN 1925

Under my lead, *House 31 operates with military precision*
  Kids rise no later than 6:30, dine 3 times daily
Take oil or medicines as ordered,
  Bathe without cursing or vulgarity
Are not permitted to smoke or gamble
  And write home month[ly]

Not that anyone on the outside writes back. I-love-you
  Must be taught in schools and shown in picture shows
More satisfying and oftentimes quicker to watch trees
  Green after winter than bear the burden of a blank page
And let its whiteness define time

There is really so little to tell
  The other teacher and I have to make the whole day up
But we never complain in front of the kids
  Instead, we amuse ourselves
With seeing the sky through their eyes

The Children's Letters from House 31

An elephant on the roof each morning
I am just getting started and hope is ~~not~~ good
After twenty-one thousand days in Carville
    Believe it or not Mr. Ripley
A kitten mothering hens was the life of the party

Mama, do not believe them
    They do not know I can be cured
If a cow can have two heads and be born at the station dairy
    I take my bath treatments regularly and say the rosary
Every evening, Hope bends her head at my window
    And ties her shoes

On a Sunday afternoon
    Eating stone permits ostriches to grind roughage
From the desert plants and hard objects they consume
    Instead of bulls, we hunt birds and gather hyssops

Miss Roma says elephant soup will keep our memory strong
    And octopus tails will give us muscles
When we can't sleep, Mr. Gabe reminds us to breathe
    Count heartbeats, he says

Folks, your hello would be a brush of leaves over a hollering creek
    On a dark night, it would be a raft of moonlight
We could fish dreams and cast away nightmares
    Remembering to breathe together

Edmond Writing to His Wife Claire

Where the ink should have spelled *I love you*
    There are so many other ways to say *I need you*
Send money, pray for me, think of me, don't worry, or *trust*
    Even an *I don't know* can substitute for love

If you listen carefully enough
    Sound, afraid of nothing, can break fences, dodge bullets,
And cross borders
    Words dressed in ink can simulate a voice in lonely quiet
Or serve as garments from the cold
    But your silence hurts

Perhaps I can understand the place you are in, the truth of it
    Two kids to raise on your own
And no proof this nightmare will wake
    Perhaps I know the futility of lending words like they're bricks
Made without straw, fearful the ground will sink from under you
    Or the walls you have built will crumble

I appreciate how light is made
    From a bulb turned on and off without encumbrance
The same with love, if we make the effort
    What is it that galaxies can travel billions of years
And still jiggle particles in our eyes

Yet from you there is no saying, no letter, no word,
    After all these months. Only indifference
Not disease but silence affects our marriage
    And the fact is, our children hear it like a snake's rattle
Hidden in grass

Gabe Michael Sees Roma's Still Life

Still fruit is hardest to draw when it wants to move
    It will trick your eye so you have to bait it with light

Moist and red, warmer than a month of Sundays
    Strawberries in a bowl and strewn on a table top

Framed among flowers, a slice of melon in the shade
    Keeps the whole scene balanced

ANOTHER LOVE

House 30 might as well have been a world away
    Roma sitting at her easel all day
Painting fruit so good Gabe Michael could taste its juice
    When he taught school

He had the boys move their desks facing west
    So he could look over their heads east
Out his window and through hers
    He lost himself in her palette, smudged with paint

Red as an apple

Gabe Michael's Canteen

The Tammany Hall of Carville became the politics not to die
    In this place. The daily struggle not to look too far past its fence
Patients lived on, in grief, blind and lame
    While loved ones on the outside sealed their tombs

Before their time, patients opened their own graves
    Brushed its dust off their clothing
And took to dreaming themselves
    Out of caskets loved ones made with the prettiest of flowers
By the time they actually died
    They were masters at defeating death

Not once, but twice, and seventy times after that
    Every day they buried themselves in something to do
From tennis to golf, baseball to music, dances to dinners
    School to *talkies*—there was already enough silence
Why watch it

When the rest of the United States divided things
    Into *white* and *colored*
Patients celebrated *35 drinking fountains, one for each cottage*
    Electrically refrigerated and without the hassle of bailing water
From a single hose. Diversity abounded
    So that even the cleaning crew was considered

Not for what they did, but who they were. They all mattered
    At Carville, not always to doctors or nuns,
And certainly not to *outsiders,* but to each other
    They could trace hands, see with eyes shut
And stock the shelves with candy bars, tobacco, and art

Sadie Morgan Spencer's Story

In 1927, Sadie's sister had tuberculosis
    And lived on her grandmother's screened porch
To gesture hello or say goodbye
    The sisters touched hands through the metal mesh
No matter what doctors said
    Or how their grandmother reproved them from her window
Before dawn and back again at night
    The sisters cackled like birds about the day

At only eight years old
    Sadie made the trek from her house to Mrs. Claire's to work
Washing dishes and laundry, pressing sheets
    And sweeping floors
Before there was enough cash in New Iberia to go around
    Mrs. Claire paid the help in food
Until her husband finally died in 1932

His ten-thousand-dollar life insurance check
    Ensured teachers in the town were paid
Through the Depression Mrs. Claire earned enough in interest
    On her loan to the city to graduate Sadie to pennies
It would be another 50 years before Sadie earned a gross
    $96 a month and $100 at Christmas

Long after her sister died
    Sadie took each day's crumbs of leftover bread to the birds
In Mrs. Claire's backyard, nothing was wasted
    Although, it could be argued, everything came too late

AFTER DEATH, LUCIE WALKS ALONG THE TRAIN TRACKS IN ST. PETER'S CEMETERY

Lucie's grave is without dates
    Therefore, she doesn't remember she is too old to be alive
For hours she waits along the train tracks
    In a casket she mistakes for a porch swing
That isn't there anymore

She has worn-out her ankle bone from gliding her foot
    Up and down her burial vault
Thinking she is on the porch that Sunday afternoon
    Before she left for Texas
It was just too much, she says
    I watched Marie and Albert grow up

Marie thought Albert was her baby doll and carried him
    Everywhere she went. Until he was almost six
When he finally refused to play dress-up
    He took a frog out of his pocket and scared her to death
She left him alone after that

Then she got sick
    I didn't notice it for a while
She didn't tell me, but I figured it out
    When she wouldn't leave her room, I knew

LUCIE AND CLAIRE'S AGREEMENT

After her death, even with concrete falling out of her mouth
    Lucie continues to dream her children into present tense
She smells plaster and wood on the porch of a house
    That no longer exists. There is solid darkness,
Hard as stone, she insists

Lucie witnessed bodies fall out of coffins, moved by the water
    That spring, in 1927, corpses could have been anyone
In New Iberia, the haunt of flesh in various states of decay
    Floated through streets and knocked on our doorsteps

Sadie said the dead nearly drove Claire crazy
    The idea of all those people returning, demanding their lots
Poverty only had to knock once for wood to rot, Claire believed
    So she bade Sadie to poke away anything
That floated to the porch

The dead never bothered Lucie
    They couldn't
By then three of her children were somewhere among them
    Claire's children were living with her

My Grandmother Leonide on Her Parents Edmond and Claire

From Daddy's death, I learned to forgive the cold of public policy
    But to remember I learned to chew injustice
And taste its bitterness down my throat
    I learned to pack the years like mud into bricks
And dam my tears in defiance
    Learned the business of life was getting through another day

With yesterday insisting on coming through the door
    I remember my grandmother Lucie curled in the fetal position
Plump and warm, she was four feet eight inches of consistency
    And earth. Her teeth ground to their roots, exposed, and in pain,
From the stone of nothing to do. Nothing to say
    I crawled on her bed and hugged her

After Mama's death, I learned a mother's love can shoot
    Through a house quicker than lightning
In death, as in life, I remember her
    Quick to speak and tossing her arms making cakes or breaking
A chicken's neck for dinner, without a blink, talking to Sadie
    Or ordering the house to keep something to do
So she wouldn't give in to the silence that fell around her

Until the day she died, Mama insisted Daddy's casket
    Had rainwater in it. She could never bring herself to dig him up
As her mother-in-law had done with Charlie
    To clutch his bones and accept the death of him
A mirror to herself and all she held dear in him
    Carrying the smell of his flesh on her hands while she baked

Telegram for Miss Claire Landry

Your husband critically ill and wants you to come immediately.
Signed U.S. Marine Hospital, Carville. December 4th 1932. 8 a.m.

During last
few hours   Sound bent forward
of life,   pressed on the window

                 through the corpse of its visit
there was twitching
of muscles   Ed heard "Daddy"
over body.   spoken in the kitchen

Edmond tried speaking
but couldn't.   He tried running
                to catch his daughter
                in backward glances

He was restless and
coughing
and lapsed into
a coma.   tried to imagine his son
Uremic poisoning.

LEONIDE REMEMBERS NORBERT'S FUNERAL, 1924

Aunt Adrienne lifted Leonide forward and shouted *"Regardez"*
  She wanted her niece to remember that
No matter what was to come
  No matter what anyone would ever tell her
There was a human in the coffin

What Leonide remembered was that the sound of *"Regardez"*
  Echoed out of the casket
As if the dead had spoken it

Fragments from the Papers of Norbert and Edmond Landry

I. September 11, 1924

Mourning's become a way of life
    A calling back (family-tried)
I'm grinding my teeth each night and can't stop
    The knowing afterwards (Norbert's doctor's notes
Not "leprosy" but *pulmonary tuberculosis*)
    Apparatus (Married: No) numerous discrete nodules
On face and lobes
    Ulcers on thighs   Unable to walk   Acid-fast stains
Race: white

II. August 8, 1919

Without proof, who will dream us awake
    Have something, at least, belong to the truth of the place
Show the world *my letter*
    When I write to one it will count for all
Swollen are the days between writing a line
    And receiving a response
By the way, I am only half myself

III. Saturday Morning, Undated

The canned chicken made us sick
  I can't keep even milk down
My feet and legs are engorged
  I have a gland under my arm the size of a head
Everything in me wants out
  And there's really no news except that

REMAINS

I.

It was 2003 when Edmond's body was exhumed
    To save him from the water Claire worried
Had his soul in unrest
    Of course his body was wet

Not from water
    But from death
Skin becomes paste

They opened his grave
    And seventy-one years brushed my face
His skull was hidden by a piece of wood
    So opaque that the timber resembled a shawl
Sunken into the haunt of his nose, mouth, eyes, lips

My grandmother Leonide and I watched as his casket fell apart
    The word "leper" written on top of it

II.

In the kitchen
    We exhumed his body a second time
Over smoke from tea with lemon

What Edmond knows, death, its brightness
    Shoveled in a garbage bag
Silent

BECOMING FLESH

DEAR FOLKS,

I don't know myself.
In here they don't use names.
On any given day, I can be
called Sisiro, Albert, or James Jackson.

I wish you could see me.
I've changed. I've grown
a mustache and wear a derby
and I've tanned.

It's all about getting in the dirt
and sweating the sickness out.
Every time I do, I feel
like a new man.

Dear Claire,

I don't expect you to understand.
Here, I am human again,
less a leper today than I've been.

It is beautiful New Orleans,

Its legs knee-deep in the Mississippi.

Reflections distorted with
Its strange personifications of humans

Spilled on the pavement.

Dear Folks,

An old fellow we are watching die
since Sunday has been talking out his head
and having convulsions. That flies aren't enough,
we are raising our hands in prayer,
but pray as we must for mercy,
I cannot ask the Lord to cure me.
I am just trying to adjust to the dead of the place,
like Lazarus in his tomb before he could tell what he had seen.

I am breathing too much in a cell that has rats,
wide-planked floors and dreams spent on looper-clips
too much smelling pine.
What is the price of the collars you sent?
By the way, the old man died.

DEAR CLAIRE,

One man was there from the outside scared of us,
not knowing what he had—and he is here today
one of us, expecting to be cured in three weeks.

Dear Folks,

The river situation is worse.
The levee has become indifferent
and I am afraid the rest of the world with it.

Things are not good here.
Carville is pregnant with a
loneliness that startles me
off of my seat sometimes.
I've tried to scream,
but nothing ever comes out
except tears.

There was a murder here last week.
One patient killed another.
And now with the levee to break,
well, I don't think I can stand it.
I will not be killed a leper.
Oh, the nuns offer their blessings
and tell me not to worry,
but prayer replaces people here.

Religion is a pastime thought interrupts.
What else would the saints do
if they didn't have a sinner to forgive
or a leper to cure?

The nuns tell me to keep my faith.
Trust.
But I don't know.
Tell Claire,
the authorities have a boat in front of the big house for *their* use.

DEAR CLAIRE,

The trouble with this place
is getting out of bed to live
through the corpse of another day;
letting the world roll as God wants it,
while we sit on the front porch
and wave flies
from our face.

Isn't it a wonder
more of us do not go crazy,
forced to live brooding over these unfortunate conditions;
thrown into a contact so intimate and prolonged
we let go our reflections in the river,
and our loved ones—but most importantly,
the very children we've begotten—
forget us.

Dear Folks,

Don't mention it.
I've just been in a rut.
Last week it was a year since
I was on a ship bound for France and today I'm here,
discharged from the army and stripped of my
citizenship.
Honorably. With Leprosy
All in the same sentence,
the same year.

Tell God he's a hypocrite
and then let everything drop dead.
That's what He wants isn't it—
or the sisters at least—an excuse for prayer?

DEAR CLAIRE,

Authorities cannot expect us to forget
we are men. A table was put in the hall
that divides us from the ladies so that
we could play cards without ever sleeping.
Stepping out of our respective places is against the rules.
Children were born early this year. You can't kill an idea.

They've built a wall that runs through the dining room
but that hasn't stopped some of the men from jumping it.
Truly, this place is a monkey cage, and none of us asked
to be here, away from our wives, and for the boys, well,
to deny them the chance at romance is a crime.

If you knew what I knew and lived as I lived,
certainly, you would understand better
the injustice of the place and who I am
as opposed to who I was.

Dear Folks,

I'll tell you what you will not find in newspapers.
Clara Mertz was going blind
and wanted to see her father for the last time
so she wrote and asked him to be on his front porch.
She assured him she would not get down or even try
to engage in conversation. She just wanted
a memory of him. Two days before she was to leave,
she received a typed letter from her father's attorney, which read:

To Whom It May Concern:
Mr. Mertz's daughter died thirty years ago.

Dear Claire,

Doctors operated on a baby yesterday,
whose pulse was 175 to 200, and all the nuns could tell me was
Don't worry. It would be a blessing if he died.
Well, I refuse to be someone's blessing.
God didn't put me here. People did.
I have legs to walk and a mouth to speak and hands to write.
The other patients are stuck in a rut of lifelessness.
They stare at walls and excuse the room for wheelchairs
as if no one is in them.

Another patient was in bed dying.
The nuns notified her only surviving niece and nephew,
and the two came as quickly as possible.
They walked in the hall, went right past Grace's room,
and asked the orderly to gather Grace's belongings.
When he took longer than they had time,
they entered her room, grabbed her jewelry box and money,
and left without even so much as a glance at their aunt in the bed.

It all makes me so mad I forget myself.
And now with the levee to break, well, I don't think
I can stand it. If a baby's death is a blessing and our belongings
are spoils, then the majority is bound to say *let them drown,*
even God is getting rid of them now.

If things get any worse,
will you or the folks come to get me and my gang?
Will you at least gather our remains from the side of the road?

Dear Folks,

A terrible thing happened here last week.
The last fellow that came in tried killing himself.
He said he was better off dead than to worry
this way. His wife is in an insane asylum
and his children are making do without either parent.
He has a sibling here too, and I regret informing him
even she is not good. Tell Claire about him.
Maybe she will understand he has spent
the better part of the day throwing up
and refuses to eat.

She has not answered any of my letters
and it's been months since I've heard from the children.
Leonide and Wilbert haunt my dreams.
Will they know enough about me that I might live in theirs?
It isn't fair.

Hotel takes anyone's money and not one's blood tests.
And there are doctors in New Orleans
who will treat even a leper.
If Claire isn't going to speak to me
or at least let me see the children,
I refuse to sit in this cell she calls a hospital room.
There's a woman here from Ecuador.
She teaches the kids to see through art,
to imagine themselves anywhere but here.
She's taught me many things I cannot unlearn,
like how to see past the hole in the fence
and dream in color and move with light.

DEAR CLAIRE,

My folks have opened their eyes to the truth of the place.
Read this clip from our newsletter. It seems
a leper died from exposure in a boxcar
while being shunted from city to city.

I can do without a home, state, and country.
But I will not do without the children.
Stay where you are if you wish.
I cannot be still anymore.

Dear Folks,

There are certain Easter dispositions I cannot sustain.
What have I done to warrant confession?
My actions have not sentenced me here.
Disease has. Ignorance has. Fear has.

Must I apologize for living?
Were I dead would I be charged with making the grave paradise?
Would I be condemned
because my spirit found a way to live anyway?
How is a man to survive alone?
Even Job had Satan to keep him company in grief.

If Claire will not see me, if she continues to keep our children
from visiting me, there may be nothing I can do about it,
but that isn't my sin.
Let her confess it, and the law after her, for putting us both in
these positions. Where both of us stand isn't where we wanted,
but it is where we are without apology.

DEAR CLAIRE,

We are *two cats*
Tied by the tail disemboweled

Thrown on either side of a fence
Doesn't mean I don't love you

I'm just so tired of hanging
With no end to it

Inherent

My View

I.

This tree is huge now
    The one in the photograph. I used to climb it
The same tree my father is running in front of
    My sisters and I built a house in the top of it
From wood and boxes we stole across the street

Our father is laughing
    I guess he was happy
Eyes shut, mouth opened, arms spread wide
    Almost looks like he's flying

I would never predict that toddler in this picture
    Grew into a man who'd try to drive into a Mack truck
Then call my mother to tell her
    The child in the front seat changed his mind

II.

Claire co-owned the family store with her brother until her death
    Her grandson, my father, labored for 90 dollars a week
Her children—my grandmother Leonide and Wilbert—inherited
    The old wood structure filled with cigarette boxes and candy

In the 1980s, at eleven million dollars in annual revenue,
    The business proved tobacco was still a cash crop,
And when you mix it with chocolate, addiction pays the best
    Residuals. My cousin says, to save a buck,
Wilbert and my grandmother mopped the worn floors
    With his cloth diapers

They encouraged workers to buy their lunch, on credit,
    From vending machines. Employees paid back, with interest,
To the company store. By Fridays, they could barely afford
    Their rent, so my family extended a favor
By letting some work weekends

III.

By 1984 my father was exhausted from working at the store
    For barely minimum wage. After he attempted suicide
My mother and grandmother had him committed
    And the two women began to talk
During the hour-long drive to the institution

My grandmother relived visiting her aunts and uncles in Carville
    She remembered her father
And the place-settings at the dining table going from 4 to 3
    Without explanation. Her mother carried out the day's chores,
Followed the letter of the law, and supplemented her income

Baking cakes and selling roses in 1924
    With Wilbert still a baby in her arms. Claire moved on
And my grandmother never forgave her for it

IV.

What I remember of my father's absence is
    The house became dark, monsters kept me up,
And stories that my mother told me were the only blankets
    Magical enough to put me to sleep

Made from a special weave of all of the past and present
    My mother recited stories Sadie had told her
Of my father's relatives and the weariness
    That had haunted them from years of separation

She showed me the photograph of my father
    When he was a toddler, chasing his laughter
Around a sapling that became the largest cedar
    In my grandmother's backyard. During the day,
My sisters and I climbed it to listen for his echo

When I Imagine My Grandmother Leonide Waiting for Her Father, Edmond, to Return

A bend in light creates a mirage, or so it seems
    Until she hits an iceberg and the whole scene falls apart
Her ship sinks and she is left in water gazing at the stars
    Hoping their warmth finds her before the sharks

My Regret

My great-grandmother's house is a place I remember
    Jumping on her bed and running marathons
Down the home's long hallway
    Her white kitchen table and side porch caught the breeze
Of roses from the yard

The dining room set for guests with a white laced cloth
    Covering its deep mahogany. The downstairs bedrooms
My cousins and I used for hide-and-seek
    The rooms upstairs we never ventured into
Because we were convinced a ghost haunted them

Children to a certain age, Sadie told us, had the gift of sight
    They could see spirits, and Mrs. Claire's house had many
Good ones, she assured us,
    But we never dared to invite them to play

When Claire and Edmond's Marriage Is Mentioned at Any Holiday Celebration

I.

Amid my father's generation and mine
    Yesteryear combusts, the turkey explodes
Opinions become sharper
    Than broken plate-shards

From the living room in photographs
    Our dead loved ones jeer us on
Each spirit takes a side
    And possesses it

The game
    Ready to begin around a carcass
Has each fact and its analysis
    Weighed

II.

On one side, there is Claire
    To her grandchildren, her memory is a steady purse of candy,
A spread of food at lunch, real butter, and donuts on Sunday

At the mention of money, those in her corner would say she was
    Cheap, thrifty, and entrepreneurial
Resolute in moving forward and not letting the past lift its head

On the other side, to anyone not blood, particularly in-laws
    Her purse was shuttered, her criticisms bitter,
And lunch with cake was something she let them eat
    Before commanding they work

III.

Next, there is Edmond's case, found in a letter
    He describes his marriage, or maybe his wife, as *dead love*

On his side, my mother says, he *never drank* or *beat her*
    But he had bruises and Claire did too
The whole house was a wound

From its opened front door, down the long center hallway,
    To the back kitchen, no amount of cleaning Sadie did
Could erase his absence or Claire's resentment

IV.

Some relatives argue the marriage of my great-grandparents
    Was a love story

They claim Claire and Edmond resolved their differences
    On his deathbed

The problem: Edmond was in a coma
    And the medical record does not account for visitors

V.

Of my father's family, my mother argues,
    Their capacity to love resembles
Mold growing on the stilled energy of fruit in a bowl

VI.

Please, bourbon and water, until next year

Lessons from a Case Study I Give My Students

I. "Report of Physicians Ordered by the Court" (1956)

Maybe the choice wasn't Ed's. For the sake of his children,
    He might have felt he had to remain in hospital
And ignorance can be excused for Norbert—after all,
    He was the first Landry to enter Carville
Regarding Amelie, modern surgical techniques
    Removed enough of her face to warrant staying
When it comes to Marie, her *status prior to expiration* is enough
    To infer why she didn't leave: First, the loss of her vision
Second, she *suffered from an unknown brain syndrome*
    Like her mother and her Aunt Pauline,
Marie existed in a coma-like disposition
    For some years she either refused to, or couldn't, speak—
One of the two or maybe both
    "Immobility," a last defense of the brain
Maybe her "frozen" state was her way of not losing
    Another thing or person

The case is different for Albert
    He had "the disease" but did not suffer from it
He only admitted to "leprosy" in 1941
    When authorities diagnosed his sister, Marie
They would have taken her at gunpoint
    From the family's farm: her only home
Instead, Albert drove her to the hospital
    Norbert, Edmond, and Amelie each died alone
But Albert stayed until her death
    That part can be explained
But after July 26, 1962, Marie's death,
    He chose to remain at the hospital
That part proves contentious

II. February 13, 1956

At Carville no one disputed that Albert came from "old money"
    Indeed, after its slaves were freed, the family had diversified
Its interests in banking, law, agriculture, and the entrepreneurial
    Spirit. As late as the mid-twentieth century, members still sold
Property to the highest bidder. For sport, across Louisiana,
    Cousins named streets after each other the way animals piss
To mark territory. Lawyers (some cousins
    And others from even "older money") finagled wills
To disenfranchise some heirs and calculated strategies
    For paying federal taxes for others
In Carville as well as outside it, family owned a bit of earth:
    A cottage on the old plantation

The hiccup to the family's financial growth came in 1956,
    When Aunt Adrienne died
Leaving 1/10th of her interests to Marie. The Estate proposed
    To subdivide some of the property for residential purposes
But the problem, the Estate determined, was Marie

What if *prospective purchasers inquir*[ed] *into the situation*
    And *reject*[ed] *the title*
Small-town rumor could be dismissed,
    But *this* potentially made her location public record
Although there is no reason to consider
    That Albert or Marie countered the Estate—in fact,
Such sells had guaranteed Marie financial security—
    It remains to be argued how she or Albert felt

If released, which relative would have let them in
    Where would they have felt wanted
Who among *the clan* would have cared for them without pity
    Possessions they could sign away, but without love,
What were they

III. August 10, 1919

Aunt Adrienne's first letter is not to her nephew Norbert
    It is to a nun at Carville to whom she addresses for advice
Tell me, she writes, is it safe for people to go visit the patients . . .
    And is there any danger to correspond with them?

Aunt Adrienne's fear is understandable for the period
    At least she asked questions rather than accept public policy
But that she needed to ask at all—that love, as an action,
    A simple letter written, was not her instinct—
May provide evidence for Uncle Albert's decision
    To remain at Carville from 1962 to his death in 1977

Edmond wrote to Claire, sometime in 1926, to tell her
    Hotel takes anyone's money and not one's blood tests
He understood wealth could take him anywhere, except home

WITH REGARDS

I.

In 1928 my great-grandfather reproached his wife
    For not visiting him. *Claire,* he wrote, *you think you are*
Unhappy now, but you have our kids, your home,
    Your daily work, and your mother
In fact you have all that you have ever had except me

But he warned her: These things are not permanent
    Your mother is *not immortal*
And the facts of my disease will come back to haunt you
    Leprosy is not contagious
And does not resemble the biblical disease

Her shunning him and keeping his children away
    He would not forget
How you refused me the little happiness that I asked of you
    One cannot do a leper an injustice and get by with it

Love, he wrote, *has no fear*

II.

For many years, I wanted so badly for Claire to have written
    One letter to Edmond
One sheet of ice to have broken from the glacier of her silence

With one response. I thought I found the rime
    In a letter Claire inscribed to her grandson in 1972
Nearly forty years after Edmond's death

She wrote of herself in third person as *the old girl*
    Who *is definitely not what she used to be*
To her disbelief, *at 75 years*

She could not imagine she *was that old*
    Except when [she] *look*[ed] *in the mirror*

Claire never considers her husband in the letter,
    But she saw herself disappearing

I hope she heard his echo in the glass,
    Reminding her nothing lasts

III.

My great-grandmother Claire widened the gulf
    Between her and her husband by convincing herself
That Edmond was *not suffering*

She trusted doctors, public health policy, and her faith
    She believed prayer and medicine would give him
Every attention during his period of treatment

And nothing swayed her from *forg*[ing] *ahead resolutely*
    Pushing his name, his memory, farther and farther
She prayed that *there* [was] *no loss in separation*

That in God everything was united
    She was resigned to *let the past go*
Her husband on the bank of the Mississippi River

She made fear her faith, *close and abiding, secure*
    In the dream of *forever,* she sealed Edmond's casket,
Cashed *three life insurance* checks, and went about her days

IV.

Even in death, Claire could not bring herself
    To be near her husband, but his disease,
Or her fear of it, cannot be the excuse my family gives her

She selected a different cemetery, arranged plots for her children,
    Their spouses, her brother, mother, and in-laws—Marie
And Albert, she tolerated near her, the latter two with leprosy

She made room for the flowers
    And fitted each headstone with concrete strips
So no one's grief would be prolonged six months to a year

She had no patience for the ground to settle, no time for anything
    Other than *keeping on* and moving
One foot in front of the other

One step to the next she gave thought to,
    Except that in her own crypt she would be lying down
The *years* she *must have slept through* a dark stone weighing her

CLAIRE AND EDMOND'S CHILDREN

I.

Wilbert died first, but that was not his final act
    Unbeknown to anyone, he bequeathed his body to science

Maybe in homage to his father, he wanted himself studied
    Some inner nerve exposed to air—unconstrained on a gurney

Perhaps he hoped some trace of the disease would be found
    Some egregious malady explained on his behalf

Maybe he refused to slumber another long night in a house
    Next to his mother, maybe the thought repulsed him

Perhaps there was light in analysis that he sought
    Some clarification in being dissected that he wanted to know

II.

After Wilbert's death, my grandmother Leonide started talking
    Every day, at 3:30, with a drink in her hand, she said more

About her parents and brother, she could not dam
    The flood of memory. From before the time
When Harriet Street was paved, she saw herself

A little girl walking through a field of buttercups,
    Hearing their voices from the screened porch, she kept looking
Behind her—disappointed

The Great Nothing, out of which the Holy One called forth
    Existence, began reclaiming her in 2007
In 2008, when my father's relatives committed her

My cousin says my grandmother cried and screamed
    Like a toddler
Each time she woke to the place and realized it wasn't home

Embedded

My sister, a counselor, says trauma is a venom that flows
  In blood vessels that swell from coagulation, and pressure slows

So intense was the pain, our grandmother ground her teeth
  Until her gums bled and it hurt to speak

Nearly 95 years of not being allowed to weep caused her hands
  To curl into fists, memory with muscle and muscle memory

The mortician had to break her finger bones
  To fit the rosary in her hand that the nun insisted she hold

Walking in New Orleans with My Sisters

We see our reflections in the buildings and watch ourselves
    In light-painted windows
Moving from one sunlit pane to another
    Our glassy ghosts disappear
Perhaps to enjoy some heaven under the sidewalk

Gabe Michael walked these same streets in 1928
    To demonstrate his disease
To doctors there, he offered to bring on himself
    A lepra fever, active tubercles, and *neuritic pains*
So they could study his syndrome

From Bourbon Street to Magazine, streetcars lull us
    With the percussion of metal
Against a backdrop of fishermen cleaning up rodents
    And hosing fish guts
Our shoes wet, our pain blank

As Ever

I.

From Carville, Ed ended his letters with the phrase *As Ever*
    Tucked in two words all of his frustrations and hopes
Being forgotten and dying, both almost consumed him
    Putting on his shoes, getting out of bed, or standing
From a writing desk

Claire's going-on as usual, her fear a mass gravity pulled
    With the strength of a mule hauling a plow next to the barn
Where Ed and his siblings played as children. My cousin killed
    Herself. In debt, addicted to anything that made her feel
Alive and connected

From her nearly empty apartment, she begged for company,
    Borrowed money from relatives, and
I have no doubt, realized their only concern was 2% interest
    Monthly. Ed pleaded for love, gave away his earnings
To those less fortunate inside Carville

Ed chose to abandon the dream of his *home*
    Whether his childhood house or the one Claire kept
For his return to the living, he elected the right to happiness,
    To be entangled in the body of a woman
With whom he could dream, collapse, and fall again

Close his eyes and know himself
    In someone else's touch
Without apology. My cousin wrote a note instead:
    Still wading through all this crap
Tell everyone hello

II.

From my perspective, shrouded in the phrase *As Ever,*
  Ed hid a code of ethics that he wanted his children
To learn, though circumstances being what they were,
  He could not have foreseen its lessons would morph,
Reach multiple descendants and pass through years

In my mind, his words are not the end of any single letter
  But the creating of worlds
His language is not the accumulation of anger
  But the release of emotion
Across a field several parcels wide and thirty acres each

One hundred years is not too long to still believe in angels
  Not the feathery creatures in some distant hereafter
But the strangers that walk along my family's fenced property
  With messages in their pockets and a glimmer in their eyes
Their need for work, their desire to strive, their gratitude for living

The casing of flesh over their bones the only home they know
  Variations of hunger, warmth, and cold their economy
From which they judge each break in their rocky steps
  The road to Ever obstructed but not impossible
Day and night, strangers travel to find rest

After a meal, a prayer answered is a house warm enough
  that they can stay away from the cold of being forgotten

EPIGENETICS

The sum of five generations is an animal
    Carrying me back to my family's farm
In a dream. On this one particular night
    I am older than forty with cloud-hair
On the spine of the animal
    I am taller than sugarcane stalks
That I pinch in the field
    Where our home used to be
There is only echo and time—
    Tracks in the mud

Sugar and pine scent the exact spot
    The beast stops, panting from its journey
Fog thickens into a wooden house
    I recognize from family photographs
Through a window
    A gas lamp illuminates a ghost woman on the porch swing
Before I hear her speaking
    Her voice is a silver-blue dawn

That scatters what is left of the fog
    Swaddles my body, suddenly
More aged than I know possible
    "Is that you, Charlie? Ed? Goodness, you are *dripping*"
And without me having seen her walk from the porch
    She helps me off the creature's hump
And onto a rocker opposite her
    She pours liquid in a cup
But the quickness with which she moves
    Has me momentarily blind

As I blink my eyelids to adjust to the strange physics
    Of a body at rest yet moving
She adds cream to my coffee
    Chatting in a lavender dress that reminds me of my aunt's:
Amelie—the ghost must hear the name when I think it,

And stops talking long enough to smile—
"Now there is a baby bird pecking its beak through the casing,
    Norbert. Don't be surprised"

"My children do not visit often
    But when they do, I'll take them in any form they travel"
"Ed, does your animal need water?
    You want another cup?" "The night is music, Marie"

The house disappears
    The coffee pours itself
The porch transforms into a pier
    And we suddenly start walking. Wooden planks
Stretch before us bordered by cattails

In the heat, the swamp bubbles,
    The animal puts its trunk in the froth,
And the woman-I-know-is-Lucie continues talking ahead of me
    I try to catch up but, with each step, I become younger
Until I need her hand to balance me
    When I start crying, she turns around and lifts me
"Push those salty drops out of your eyes, Albert,
    And put them in your pocket
We will save those beady rocks for skipping
    So we can see which one reaches farthest"

Later, in the dream, we flick the tears from our hands,
    And every other one becomes an ostrich
Sprinting so quickly it seems to fly over the water—
    A feathery ball into the forest—unfurling

List of Relations

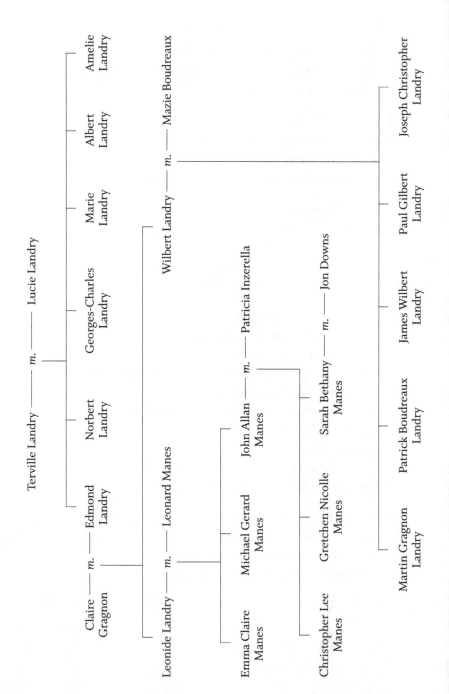

Notes

I tell this story from my vantage point as Edmond Landry's great-grandson. There are others in the family who see the events from a different perspective, especially concerning the marriage of Claire and Edmond. There is some evidence for both sides of that argument. For example, in an undated letter titled "Friday Night," Edmond writes to his folks that he "had been getting letters from Claire regularly." This contradicts other letters Edmond wrote about his wife's lack of written communication. It may be that he is softening the truth for the sake of his parents, or it may be there is a period when Claire did correspond with him. I hope I have allowed the reader a glimpse of the many differing ways family members interpret the tragic events of the past.

Between 1998 and 2003, I had the shared possession of a trove of family letters, mostly written by my paternal grandmother's uncle Norbert and her father Edmond Landry during their incarceration at the National Leprosarium in Carville, Louisiana. Today, most of these letters are archived at the University of Louisiana at Lafayette under the title "Edmond G. and Norbert T. Landry Papers, Collection 332." In 2003, I made photocopies of the collection, at that time consisting of both family letters and medical transcripts, before returning it to my grandmother (Leonide), who had been lent the assortment by her nephew (my cousin) Martin Landry. Some poems were written during those years. Others have been newly written or revised based on those photocopies. In this book, if a letter used is currently in Collection 332, then it has been credited to that archive, but if it is one of those documents, not a part of the university's file, then it has been attributed to the poet's copies.

"Tall Tales Grow Limbs, My Mother Said" opens with "In the Beginning" from chapter 7 of Stanley Stein's *Alone No Longer: The Story of a Man Who Refused to Be One of the Living Dead!*, written with Lawrence G. Blochman (1963; Carville, LA: The Star, reprinted in 1974). Zachary Gussow's *Leprosy, Racism, and Public Health: Social Policy in Chronic Disease Control* (Boulder: Westview Press, 1989) describes the religious, social, and political ideologies that affected the leprosarium. In *Miracle at Carville* (Garden City, NY: Doubleday, 1950), Betty Martin explains that patients intentionally used alternate monikers for the disease. One of those names was "it." The first stanza includes some wording from Kurt Andrew Slauson's 1995 thesis at the University of Montana, entitled "To Liberate the Particular: Politics and Poetics in Charles Olson's *The Maximus Poems.*" The second stanza is inspired, in part, by Jonathan Hutchinson's "fish theory" that was largely disputed in the late 1800s, but the phobia of eating fish and its association with "leprosy" persisted. A May 1994 *Los Angeles Times* article by Janet McConnaughey mentions that the original seven patients, sent to the leprosarium in 1894, journeyed "under the pretext of starting an ostrich farm."

"The Book of Names" lists aliases that Norbert, Edmond, and Amelie assumed in Carville to protect themselves and the Landry family from stigma. Patients were not compelled by law to choose aliases, but before the mid-1940s, the culture of the hospital strongly encouraged the practice, which Stein describes in *Alone No Longer*, 36–37. The dates that the Landry siblings were incarcerated, from entrance into Carville to their individual deaths, were these: Norbert, 1919–1924; Edmond, 1924–1932; Amelie, 1933–1940; Marie, 1941–1962; and Albert, 1941–1977.

"Public Law" is based on US Senate Bill 4086, "A Bill to Provide for the Care and Treatment of Persons Afflicted with Leprosy and to Prevent the Spread of Leprosy in the United States" (Washington DC: Government Printing Office, 15 February 1916); the Public Health Service's Code of Federal Regulations (CFR), title 42, paragraph 32.86, "Admissions to Service Facilities"; and my interview of political scientist Janet E. Frantz at the University of Louisiana at Lafayette in 2000. Frantz and Hajime Sato's 2005 essay "Termination of the Leprosy Isolation Policy in the US and Japan: Science, Policy Changes, and the Garbage Can Model," published in *BMC International Health and Human Rights Journal,* informs the last lines. First stanza italics are from two letters—one from director of Iberia Parish's health unit C. L. Mengis (10 June 1941) and the second from surgeon G. H. Faget (12 June 1941) (photocopies in the possession of the poet)—that discuss the "procedure" for confining patients to Carville in the suspected diagnosis of Marie B. Landry. Lines about ostriches, which are italicized in this poem and elsewhere in the book, come from *Compton's Pictured Encyclopedia*, vol. 10 (Chicago: F. E. Compton, 1961), 508–509.

"This House Is Sick, Sadie Told My Mother" recounts stories Sadie Morgan Spencer and Zenobia Racely told my mother (Patricia) in the late 1970s and early 1980s. Claire Landry's accounting book, dated 1981–1982 (see note for "With Regards" for how the poet acquired this source), does not list amounts she and her successors paid Sadie or Zenobia. The record shows payments of $24 Claire made to another woman who worked for her. It is highly unlikely that Sadie and Zenobia would have made sums higher than what is logged. Sadie's words about the Landrys' house being "sick" may have been literal, since there was a rumor among some of my relatives "as to the danger involved to the public in using lumber and furniture from the former home of Mr. Terville Landry" (family correspondence, 31 July 1947, poet's copy). No relative lived in the house after Albert and Marie abandoned it to take their mother (Lucie) to Port Arthur, Texas, before they entered Carville. In 1928, my great-grandfather Edmond wrote to his wife Claire, in which, among other important statements, he tried pleading the notion that the bacteria causing "leprosy," although contagious, was nothing to dread. Despite his efforts, family fears of his childhood home and its contents in 1947 suggest that Claire did not view "this discussion in the same light as" her husband (quote from Edmond, 1928). A copy of Edmond's first page to this letter is scanned in *Out of the Shadow of Leprosy: The Carville Letters and Stories of the Landry Family*, by Emma Claire Manes (Edmond and Claire's eldest grandchild) (Jackson: University Press of Mississippi, 2013), 92. See further discussion related to this 18-page letter in my notes for "Edmond Writing to His Wife Claire," "When Claire and Edmond's Marriage Is Mentioned at Any Holiday Celebration," and "With Regards." A letter to the "Medical Officer in Charge," typed or, most likely, dictated by my great-great-aunt Amelie Landry, contains "instructions in the event of death" and expresses her last written requests, the last of which reads: "With the money that I have in bank in my sister's [Marie's] name I wish to have purchased a copper-lined casket (I do not want to be put in a big box)." Dated 19 September 1940, this letter was signed using her Carville name: Emma Lee Michael (poet's copy of Amelie's letter).

"From the Grave, Lucie Orchestrates Her Memories" is based on stories told to me by my grandmother Leonide (Edmond and Claire's daughter) and Sadie, who worked for my grandmother after Claire's death in 1981. The two women told me "Charlie" was buried somewhere on our family farm. Since then, his very existence has been the source of dispute between myself and some relatives. Records from St. Peter's Catholic Church in New Iberia list Georges-Charles Landry as the son of Terville and Lucie (29 October 1896 to 25 March 1897). Church files do not indicate where he is buried, which may support the story that he was interred on family property. I was told "Charlie" had been the first child born of my great-great-grandparents (Terville and Lucie Landry), but the current record does not reflect that chronology. The last two stanzas use wording from two sources. The first source is Amelie's note to the "Medical Officer in Charge" (see note for "This House Is Sick, Sadie Told My Mother"). The second source, "Ward Surgeon's Progress and Treatment Record," describes "the massive nodular involvement around [Amelie's] mouth" as a "button-hole mouth" due to the "many repetitions of ulceration and healing." This latter paper, dated the day she died, 24 September 1940, lists a chronology of her medical care from 1923 to 1940. One entry explains that Amelie "could scarcely eat any solid food. This prevented dental care, and eventually some of her teeth became carious and the gums infected." Despite a 1938 surgery to make "eating and drinking . . . easier for a while," "the ulcerations and scarring began again" and, in January 1939, she became "bedfast" and "had an almost continuous shower of tubercles, some open, some closed." Photocopies of Amelie's letter and the ward surgeon's paper are with the poet. Original medical records of most former Carville patients are at the National Hansen's Disease (Leprosy) Program in Baton Rouge, Louisiana.

"Edmond, Writing under His Carville Name Gabe Michael, in 1925" excerpts lines, in the first stanza, from "Rules for Kids House 31," written on 19 August 1925 and signed by Gabe Michael. My great-grandfather was in charge of the boys at Carville until, he told his folks, they were old enough to be placed in the "men['s] houses" (13 October 1929), but a letter to Dr. O. E. Denny on 15 October 1929 contradicts that reason. In that latter correspondence, Edmond writes "that none of the boys[sic] room was in order." He explains that the disorder of the boys' room was because he thought "that we were all to move to house 41." The boys did not graduate to the men's quarters. Edmond's (Gabe Michael's) duties were stopped. The differing accounts provide one example that not all of the correspondences between Edmond and his parents were completely truthful. He may have censored his writing to protect them or himself. Edmond's letters are a part of Collection 332. The last two stanzas are the poet's own imaginings.

"The Children's Letters from House 31" (lines 1, 3–5, and 8) uses excerpts from the leprosarium's newsletter, *The Sixty-Six Star* (1931–1934). Original copies of the newsletter are archived at the National Hansen's Disease Museum in Louisiana. *Carville Legacies: Recipes and Recollections* lists elephant and octopus among favorite dishes remembered by patients, Carville volunteers, or hospital staff. In the cookbook there is a story, recounted by Bliss Morris, about a stranger who goes from one home to another begging for food, but on each door that he knocks the inhabitants say they have nothing to eat, and it soon becomes clear that the entire community is "irritable with one another" from hunger (31). Desperate for food, the stranger goes to the park, takes a rock, washes it, and places it in a pot of water that he has someone fetch. He invites another person to start a fire, and they boil the rock. As more people gather, he encourages them to search their homes and grounds for any ingredient they can find. One neighbor brings a cabbage, another a few potatoes, and one offers salt. A leftover chicken wing and neck are added to the pot, too, and soon the citizens feast over the stranger's "Rock Soup." The parable ends with a lesson: "Collaboration works Magic" (31). This story inspired me to insert lines 13 and 14 from a passage in *Compton's Pictured Encyclopedia,* which my grandmother Leonide used to read to me when I was a child. Italics in the first two stanzas take words or similar phrasing from Collection 332. "Hyssops" is a biblical term used in ritual purification of "lepers" (Leviticus 14:52 and Psalm 51:7). A short analysis of *Tzara'at,* a Hebrew word of unknown origin and often mistranslated as "leprosy," can be found before Leviticus 13 in W. Gunther Plaut's edited version of *The Torah: A Modern Commentary* (New York: Union of American Hebrew Congregations, 1981), 828–30. "Hollering creek" is from a short story by Sandra Cisneros, "Woman Hollering Creek."

"Edmond Writing to His Wife Claire" is based on family gossip about a letter, long removed from Edmond's papers prior to 1998. I was told Edmond's missing letter included details that he had met a South American woman and considered escaping Carville with her. Most lines in this poem were written between 1998 and 2003 when no physical evidence of this incident existed, but there were possible inferences of it from some of Edmond's correspondences to his folks: one dated 16 February 1927 and another on 27 August 1928. In the first paragraph of these notes, I reference an undated letter titled "Friday Night," in which Edmond contradicts several of his letters to and about Claire, concerning her apparent refusal to write to him. In that letter, he writes his parents that he "had been getting letters from Claire regularly."

These letters are part of Collection 332. A long letter, which details problems in Edmond and Claire's marriage, was found by a relative in 2008. In an email to family, that relative announced, "I think it is 'the' missing letter." That year, my requests to view it were unanswered, but in *Out of the Shadow of Leprosy,* Emma Claire Manes describes the letter as consisting of 18 pages and includes a transcription of those pages (93–123). As of 15 December 2018, this letter has not been archived in Collection 332, nor have I seen the copy found in 2008. Therefore, I cannot confirm if this letter is the one rumored to have been removed from the collection prior to 1998 or if it is different.

"Gabe Michael Sees Roma's Still Life" is based on a painting of fruit given to me by Mary Ruth, a patient at Carville. The artist's signature appears to read "Roma," but I have come to learn that there was a painter there by the last name of "Romo," so this piece may be by her. To my knowledge, this patient never knew Edmond.

"Gabe Michael's Canteen" refers to a business my great-grandfather started, which came to be called "a minor-league Tammany Hall" (Stein, *Alone No Longer*, 61). The politics at Carville was not limited to the store's operations. Religion and the management of the hospital itself were regular sources of dispute. Edmond writes to his folks, "We have prayers every day this month. The Catholic part of my gang surely hates the idea. But if they miss prayers they have to miss a show so they are very punctual" (2 October 1925). In an undated letter, Edmond notes that some of the patients "want to put the sisters and the priest out [and] others a[re] petitioning to have Dr. W. fire[d]." Edmond worked, in the store and out, to move patients from their "deadly lethargy" (Stein's words about Edmond/Gabe Michael, 53). June and July 1934 issues of *The Sixty-Six Star* mention different notes about the expected thirty-five "Drinking Fountains," "Modernizing Certain Bathrooms," and, overall, the "New Construction" happening in the hospital. These restorations would have been made after Edmond/Gabe Michael's death, but they would have been improvements to Amelie's living conditions inside the infirmary. In one of my conversations with Mary Ruth in the early 2000s, she told me about an accident involving some of the people who cleaned the hospital. That she knew their names and stories, although she had not been a patient in Carville at the time that the accident occurred in the early 1930s, impressed me. Stein also discusses the importance of cafeteria staff, who served as middlemen between the patients and "outside" services (*Alone No Longer*, 138). Stein's discussion is evidence that conditions being what they were inside the hospital, the cleaning crew and cooks may have had more resources and, therefore, a higher social standing than domestic workers on the "outside."

"Sadie Morgan Spencer's Story" remembers Sadie's sister Gracie Morgan, who died of tuberculosis. In Sadie's lifetime, she buried four of her five children. Sadie refused to give death power in silence. She spoke of her children and sister often. To her, Gracie was alive in spirit and looking after her deceased sons (Joseph, Calvin, and Leroy) and daughter (Virda).

I wrote "Lucie and Claire's Agreement" and most of the flood imagery in the book after examining a collection of photographs of the 1927 Mississippi River flood taken either by my great-great-aunt Marie Landry or by someone from her "gang." Photographs are in the possession of the poet. In the early 2000s, Sadie moved from New Iberia to reside with her daughter out-of-state. Before she left, Sadie thought she was on a ship, fearful that its floors would break and snakes would empty out of it. My grandmother Leonide told her she was hallucinating, but when Sadie would have been eight years old and working for Claire Landry during the 1927 flood, she had to sit on the porch and poke away snakes and anything else that emerged out of the water encroaching on the street. I wonder if, in her older age, she confused my great-grandmother's house with a ship of snakes.

"Telegram for Miss Claire Landry" was sent on 4 December 1932, the day Edmond died. Italics beside the verses are from his medical papers. The telegram was telephoned to Baton Rouge, Louisiana, by a Mr. Gleason at 8:00 a.m. There is no record of the time Claire received it, but Edmond's "Clinical Record" indicates "early this morning he lapsed into a coma." He was pronounced dead at 6:45 p.m. Photocopies are in the possession of the poet. See the note for the poem "With Regards" for quotes from Claire's letter to Dr. Johansen a few days after her husband's death.

"Fragments from the Papers of Norbert and Edmond Landry" includes phrases from Norbert's medical reports in section I (poet's copy). Italics in sections II and III indicate wording from Norbert and Edmond's letters, archived in Collection 332.

"Remains" is based, in part, on my memory and personal photographs of the exhumation of Edmond Landry on February 11–12, 2003. I was present during the entire disinterment including his reburial on February 13. My grandmother Leonide (Edmond's daughter) and I witnessed his casket fall apart and were able to touch his remains. On the second night of his exhumation, before his tomb was resealed, my grandmother, mother, and I took, from the cemetery, the garbage bag in which the caretakers had placed his body, and gathered his remains in a cloth sheet. We did the best we could to bury him with materials we had: a container, which we decorated with names of our then-living relatives, an angel ornament, and roses from our backyard.

——•◆•——

The section of poetry entitled "Becoming Flesh" is based on multiple correspondences written by Norbert and Edmond Landry during their individual incarcerations at the leprosarium: Norbert from 1919 to 1924 and Edmond from 1924 to 1932. The original letters used to create these poems are listed below and are a part of Collection 332. In the case that a letter is used repeatedly, it is only listed once in this note.

Edmond to his wife (Claire Landry), 28 April 1927
Norbert to his mother (Lucie Landry), 15 August 1919
Norbert to his mother, 20 August 1920
Norbert to his mother, 18 February 1921
Norbert to his brother (Edmond), 14 January 1920
Edmond to his folks (Terville and Lucie Landry), 14 March 1928
Edmond to his wife, 28 April 1927
Edmond to his folks, 8 August 1927
Edmond to his folks, 11 January 1926
Norbert to his mother, 1 September 1919
Norbert to his mother, 1 February 1920
Edmond to his folks, 5 November 1926

"I don't expect you to understand" rephrases a line from a review of the movie *Tarzan: The Ape Man*, which was reviewed in *The Sixty-Six Star* on 7 January 1933. In it, actor Johnny Weissmuller is described as "a vivid personification of the strange human being, who was raised by the great apes as one of their own." The movie was released 2 April 1932.

"The trouble with this Place" excerpts lines from David Palmer's article in *The Sixty-Six Star* entitled "Looking Out from Within." In it are these lines,

"Forced to live brooding over these unfortunate conditions; thrown into a contact so intimate and prolonged that it would make enemies of best friends . . . isn't it a wonder that we do not . . . disembowel each other? that more of us do not go crazy? more take their own lives . . . ?" Wording from this same source also comprises the last poem in this section, the first line of which begins, "We are *two cats*." In both poems, words italicized belong to David Palmer.

"I'll tell you what you will not find in newspapers" is partially based on a story told to me by Mary Ruth. Clara Mertz was not the name of the person in Mary's story, but a woman by that name was one of the first patients to enter Carville according to the New Orleans *Daily Picayune* of 2 December 1894. In her book *Carville: Remembering Leprosy in America* (Jackson: University Press of Mississippi, 2004), Marcia Gaudet recounts a story about a woman named Rita (45–48), who Mary Ruth may have been referring to. The two stories are different but have enough in common that they may be interrelated.

"Doctors operated on a baby yesterday" excerpts some words and sentiments from Edmond's letters but mostly derives from conversations I had with Mary Ruth in the early 2000s.

"My View" uses annual revenue and a quote from my cousin, Paul Landry, found in a *Times of Acadiana* newspaper article, in which the Landry-Manes family-owned business, Gragnon's Wholesale, was listed in the "top 25 privately held companies of 1994."

"When Claire and Edmond's Marriage Is Mentioned at Any Holiday Celebration," section III, italicizes words from my great-grandfather's June 1928 letter (see note for "Edmond Writing to His Wife Claire"). In 2008, before it was transcribed and published by my father's sister (Emma Claire

Manes), a cousin sent me short quotes and paraphrases. My cousin explained that, in the letter, "Edmond talks about 'Dead Love'" and a girl named "Priseilla" (possibly my cousin's spelling since my aunt spells the child's name differently), who had been "discharged and sent up North to live with someone." Edmond wanted his wife Claire to take the child. He also wanted her and their children to move closer to the leprosarium. My cousin's email raised more questions than it answered. Who was "Priseilla"? Was her mother the woman he was rumored to have loved? Was there an ulterior motive for Edmond wanting the child near? Was she his? Did my great-grandmother deny "Priseilla" a home because the girl had been in the leprosarium or was Claire's rejection geared for her husband?

"Lessons from a Case Study I Give My Students" italicizes words from the "Report of Physicians Appointed by the Court" regarding Marie B. Landry. The paper copy is not signed, but Dr. Wolcott (clinical director) and Dr. Wood (assistant surgeon) are listed as the "undersigned Physicians." It is not dated, but a letter by the Landry-Manes family attorney mentions receipt of the report on 12 March 1956. On 7 March 1956, Dr. Rolla Wolcott also references the document. The line regarding "immobility" is quoted from Peter A. Levine's *Waking the Tiger: Healing Trauma* (Berkeley, CA: North Atlantic Books, 1997) in the opening chapter, "Shadows from a Forgotten Past," 15–17. February 13, 1956, is the date that the family's attorney, on behalf of my grandmother (Leonide) and her brother (Wilbert), formally asked Dr. Wolcott for an examination "of Miss Marie B. Landry's present condition." The letter's second-to-last paragraph states their purpose: "We will need to have information establishing that because of her condition, Miss Marie B. Landry is incapable of taking care of any properties or interests that belong to her." On page 5 of their article "Termination of the Leprosy Isolation Policy," Frantz and Sato mention that, by the 1950s, if a patient could demonstrate financial independence then "twelve negative monthly tests were no longer required for discharge." The second stanza of section II uses quotes and paraphrases from this same two-page letter (February 13). Albert's clinical record, following his death on 26 October 1977, chronicles a "Narrative Summary" of his medical history, dated 9 December 1977, in which it confirms he "had inactive lepromatous leprosy" since 7 August 1958. Copies of the letters concerning Marie, and Albert's clinical records, are in the possession of the poet. Aunt Adrienne's letter to Norbert is included in Collection 332.

"With Regards" uses five documents, mostly in this order: words from Edmond's June 1928 letter to my great-grandmother, transcribed on pages 114–15 of *Out of the Shadow of Leprosy* (see prior notes for "Edmond Writing to His Wife Claire" and "When Claire and Edmond's Marriage Is Mentioned at Any Holiday Celebration"); an August 1972 letter Claire wrote one of her grandsons; a letter of condolence from Dr. Johansen on 7 December 1932; Edmond's letter to Claire dated 28 April 1927; and "an earnest prayer," which was one of my great-grandmother's favorite supplications. In Edmond's letter to his wife on 28 April 1927 he reminds her that he "never liked levees." Dr. Johansen's letter concludes with the line, "I trust it will be a comfort to you to know that your husband received every attention during his period of treatment here." Claire responded to his letter with a handwritten note, the first line of which begins, "Three insurance companies request certified death certificates, and I would like to know if you would mail them to me. If not, kindly inform me what steps must be taken to secure these." Her next paragraph begins, "Thank you for your kind letter. It is a comfort to me, I assure you. We are greatly relieved to know that Edmond is not suffering." Claire's August letter to her grandson does not consider her husband directly, but, in the poem's second section, I use her words to imagine whether or not she did. Claire's August letter and a postcard from Martin Landry to her that same month/year (see note for "As Ever") were found by me in her accounting book. Her book had been in the attic of our family store, Gragnon's Wholesale, which my great-uncle Wilbert (Claire's son) had me empty, one summer in the 1990s, so I could burn old files and make space for new ones. Under his watchful eyes, I managed to burn the boxes that the files were in but kept some of the accounting books. It was not until 2017 that I realized my great-grandmother's accounting book had the postcard and letter stuck between two of the pages. Other than Edmond's letter to his wife, dated June 1928, these copies are in the possession of the poet. Edmond's April letter to Claire is in Collection 332.

"Walking in New Orleans with My Sisters" is based, in part, on a letter from Edmond to Dr. O. E. Denny, 29 February 1928. "Pain blank" are words from a line by Emily Dickinson: "Pain has an element of blank."

"As Ever" italicizes phrases from a postcard my cousin Martin Landry wrote his grandmother (Claire Landry) on Tuesday, 1 August 1972. Not quoted in the poem are Martin's words: "I'm rolling up a nice bankroll (but that's immaterial!?!) Hope you're holding down the fort down there [and] feeling fine. . . . give Sadie a BIG KISS!!" Claire's response to this note, eight days later, offers a reason for his tone. "Martin," she explains, "doesn't think too highly of himself except as a financier." Collectively, Martin and Claire's words may offer a way of understanding trauma's effects on my family. Business was everything and "immaterial." Work, and the pull to do it, did not provide relatives peace or meaning, but it may have been a way of "keeping on." Martin died of natural causes, but a cousin, related to me by marriage, did commit suicide in 2014. See note for "With Regards" for how the poet came to have these documents.

"Epigenetics" uses the image of an animal inspired by Ralph Waldo Emerson's "The Poet" (published 1844). "Dripping" is an ancient word for pain according to Anne Carson's note on Sappho's poetry in *If Not, Winter: Fragments of Sappho* (New York: Vintage Books, 2002), 365.

CPSIA information can be obtained
at www.ICGtesting.com
Printed in the USA
LVHW092237230120
644669LV00001B/340